Flatbush Avenue, looking south to Church Avenue, 1909. (*Eagle* Collection, Brooklyn Public Library, Brooklyn Collection.)

From *Old Brooklyn Photo Postcards* © 1983 by Dover Publications, Inc.

The Crescent Athletic Club Boat House, Shore Road, 1903. (*Eagle* Collection, Brooklyn Public Library, Brooklyn Collection.)

From *Old Brooklyn Photo Postcards* © 1983 by Dover Publications, Inc.

The Barrel of Fun, Steeplechase Park, Coney Island, 1953. (*Eagle* Collection, Brooklyn Public Library, Brooklyn Collection.)

From *Old Brooklyn Photo Postcards* © 1983 by Dover Publications, Inc.

Traffic on Flatbush Avenue near Fulton and Nevins Streets, 1927. (*Eagle* Collection, Brooklyn Public Library Brooklyn Collection.)

From *Old Brooklyn Photo Postcards* © 1983 by Dover Publications, Inc.

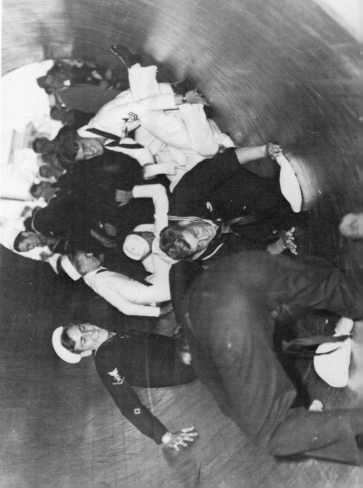

Williamsburgh branch, Brooklyn Public Library, 474 Bedford Avenue, 1901. (Brooklyn Public Library Brooklyn Collection.)

Flatbush Avenue near Church Avenue, from the steeple of the Flatbush Dutch Reformed Church, 1874. (G. B. Brainard Collection, neg. 309, Brooklyn Public Library Brooklyn Collection.)

Sands and Navy Streets, ca. 1900. (*Eagle* Collection, Brooklyn Public Library Brooklyn Collection.)

Trolleys, Nostrand and Atlantic Avenues, 1896. (*Eagle* Collection, Brooklyn Public Library Brooklyn Collection.)

Belmont Avenue Market, Brownsville, 1910. (I. Underhill Collection, neg. B16608, Brooklyn Public Library Brooklyn Collection.)

Launch of the U.S.S. *Missouri*, Brooklyn Navy Yard, January 30, 1944. (*Eagle* Collection, Brooklyn Public Library Brooklyn Collection.)

Abraham and Straus department store, Fulton Street, 1944. (*Eagle* Collection, Brooklyn Public Library Brooklyn Collection.)

The Brooklyn Bridge and Fulton Ferry House, ca. 1900. (Brooklyn Public Library Brooklyn Collection.)

Brooklyn Daily Eagle Building, Johnson and Washington Streets, ca. 1925. (*Eagle* Collection, Brooklyn Public Library Brooklyn Collection.)

From *Old Brooklyn Photo Postcards* © 1983 by Dover Publications, Inc.

The Bowery, Coney Island, ca. 1900. (E. Wemlinger Collection, Brooklyn Public Library Brooklyn Collection.)

From *Old Brooklyn Photo Postcards* © 1983 by Dover Publications, Inc.

Marathon race over the Brooklyn Bridge, 1951. (*Eagle* Collection, Brooklyn Public Library Brooklyn Collection.)

From *Old Brooklyn Photo Postcards* © 1983 by Dover Publications, Inc.

The first beer delivery after the repeal of Prohibition leaves the Trommer Brewery, Bushwick Avenue and Conway Street, 1933. (*Eagle* Collection, Brooklyn Public Library Brooklyn Collection.)

From *Old Brooklyn Photo Postcards* © 1983 by Dover Publications, Inc.